British Library Cataloguing in Publication Data

The Hippopotamus's birthday and other poems about animals and birds.
1. Poetry in English, 1945- Anthologies—For children
I. Jennings, Linda M. (Linda Marion), *1937-*   II. Hughes, Roger, *1948-*
821′.914′0809282

ISBN 0-340-43120-2

First published 1987 by Hodder and Stoughton Children's Books
This edition first published 1988 by Picture Knight
Second Impression 1988

Published by Hodder and Stoughton Paperbacks,
a division of Hodder and Stoughton Ltd,
Mill Road, Dunton Green, Sevenoaks, Kent TN13 2YE
Editorial office: 47 Bedford Square, London WC1B 3DP

Printed in Great Britain by Cambus Litho, East Kilbride

THE HIPPOPOTAMUS'S
BiRTHDAY

and other Poems about Animals and Birds

Illustrated by ROGER HUGHES

Compiled by Linda M. Jennings

Picture Knight

The Hippopotamus's Birthday

He has opened all his parcels
    but the largest and the last,
His hopes are at their highest
    and his heart is beating fast.
Oh happy Hippopotamus
    what lovely gift is here?
He cuts the string. The world stands still.
    A pair of boots appear.

Oh little Hippopotamus
    the sorrows of the small.
He dropped two tears to mingle
    with the flowing Senegal —
And the 'Thank you' that he uttered
    was the saddest ever heard
In the Senegambian jungle
    from the mouth of beast or bird.

E. V. Rieu

The Kangaroo

Old Jumpety-Bumpety-Hop-and-Go-One
Was lying asleep on his side in the sun.
This old kangaroo, he was whisking the flies
(With his long glossy tail) from his ears and his eyes.
Jumpety-Bumpety-Hop-and-Go-One
Was lying asleep on his side in the sun,
Jumpety-Bumpety-Hop.

Anon.

If I had a Donkey

If I had a donkey
That wouldn't go,
D'you think I'd wallop him?
No! No! No!
I'd put him in a stable
And keep him nice and warm,
The best little donkey
That ever was born,
Gee up, Neddy,
Gee up, Neddy,
The best little donkey
That ever was born.

Nursery Rhyme

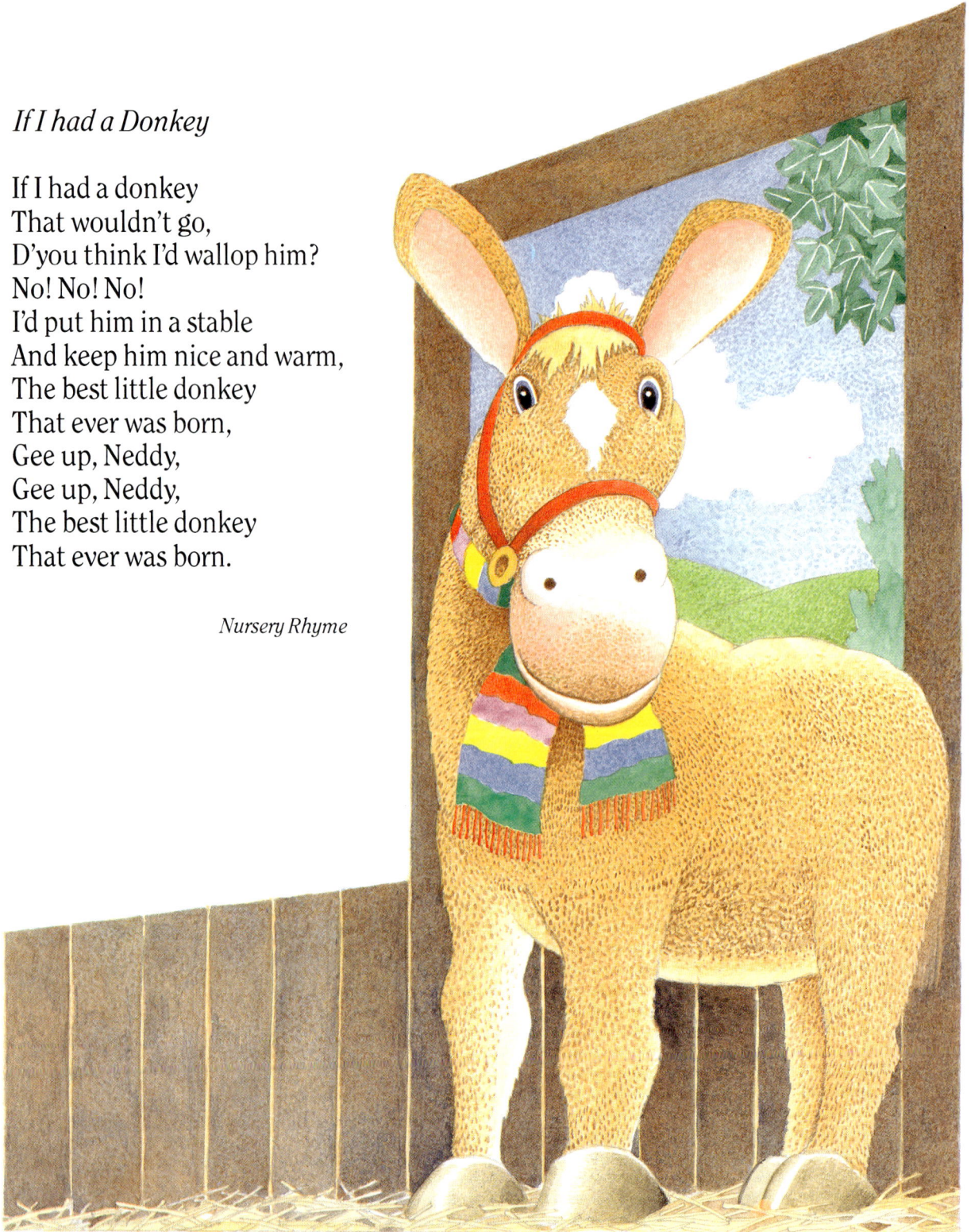

Toucans Two

Whatever one toucan can do
is sooner done by toucans two,
and three toucans (it's very true)
can do much more than two can do.

And toucans numbering two plus two can
manage more than all the zoo can.
In short, there is no toucan who can
do what four or three or two can.

Jack Prelutsky

Sunning

Old Dog lay in the summer sun
Much too lazy to rise and run.
He flapped an ear
At a buzzing fly —
He winked a half-opened
Sleepy eye.
He scratched himself
On an itching spot —
As he dozed on the porch
When the sun was hot.
He whimpered a bit
From force of habit,
While he lazily dreamed
Of chasing a rabbit.
But Old Dog happily lay in the sun,
Much too lazy to rise and run.

James S. Tippett

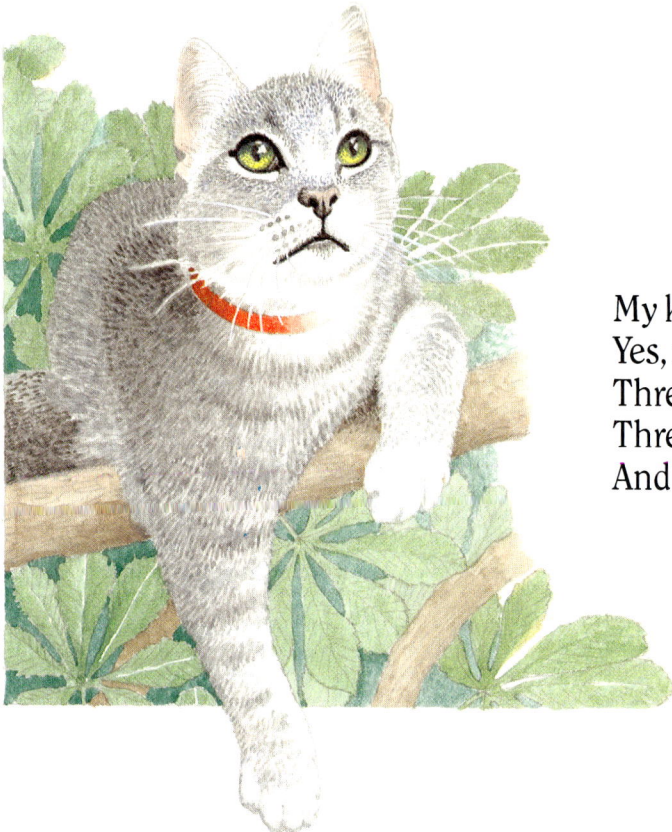

My kitty-cat has nine lives,
Yes, nine long lives has she —
Three to spend in eating,
Three to spend in sleeping,
And three to spend up in the chestnut tree.

Anon.

The Petshop

If I had a hundred pounds to spend,
  Or maybe a little more,
I'd hurry as fast as my legs would go
  Straight to the Petshop door.

I wouldn't say, 'How much for this or that?'
  'What kind of a dog is he?'
I'd buy as many as rolled an eye,
  Or wagged a tail at me.

I'd take the hound with the drooping ears
  That sits by himself alone —
Cockers and Cairns and wobbly pups
  For to be my very own.

I might buy a parrot all red and green,
  And the monkey I saw before,
If I had a hundred pounds to spend,
  Or maybe a little more.

Rachel Field

The Owl and the Pussy Cat

The Owl and the Pussy Cat went to sea
    In a beautiful pea-green boat.
They took some honey and plenty of money
    Wrapped up in a five-pound note.
The Owl looked up to the stars above,
    And sang to a small guitar,
'O lovely Pussy, Oh Pussy, my love,
    What a beautiful Pussy you are,
      You are,
      You are,
    What a beautiful Pussy you are!

Pussy said to the Owl, 'You elegant fowl,
    How charmingly sweet you sing!
Oh! let us be married — too long we have
tarried
    But what shall we do for a ring?'
They sailed away, for a year and a day,
    To the land where the bong-tree grows —
And there in a wood a Piggy-wig stood
    With a ring at the end of his nose,
      His nose,
      His nose,
With a ring at the end of his nose.

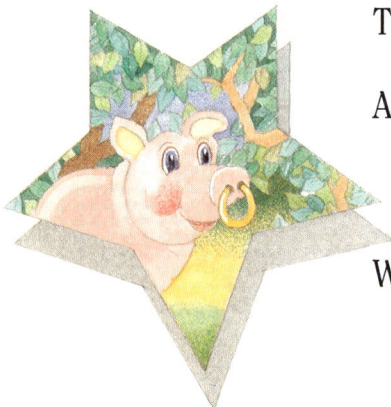

'Dear Pig, are you willing to sell for one shilling
    Your ring?' Said the Piggy, 'I will.'
So they took it away, and were married next day
    By the turkey who lives on the hill.
They dined on mince and slices of quince,
    Which they ate with a runcible spoon —
And hand in hand, on the edge of the sand,
    They danced by the light of the moon,
        The moon,
        The moon,
They danced by the light of the moon.

Edward Lear

I had a Little Pony

I had a little pony
    His name was Dapple-grey
I lent him to a lady,
    To ride a mile away.

She whipped him, she lashed him,
    She drove him through the mire.
I wouldn't lend my pony now,
    For all the lady's hire.

Anon.

The Owl

When cats run home and light is come
    And dew is cold upon the ground,
And the far-off stream is dumb,
    And the whirring sail goes round,
    And the whirring sail goes round —
      Alone and warming his five wits,
      The white owl in the belfry sits.

When merry milkmaids click the latch,
    And rarely smells the new-mown hay,
And the cock hath sung beneath the thatch
    Twice or thrice his roundelay,
    Twice or thrice his roundelay —
      Alone and warming his five wits,
      The white owl in the belfry sits.

Alfred, Lord Tennyson

Ducks Ditty

All along the backwater,
Through the rushes tall,
Ducks are a-dabbling,
Up tails all!

Ducks' tails, drakes' tails.
Yellow feet a-quiver,
Yellow bills all out of sight
Busy in the river!

Slushy green undergrowth
Where the roach swim —
Here we keep our larder,
Cool and full and dim.

Everyone for what he likes!
We like to be
Heads down, tails up,
Dabbling free!

High in the blue above
Swifts whirl and call —
We are down a-dabbling,
Up tails all!

Kenneth Grahame

Choosing their Names

Our old cat has kittens three —
What do you think their names should be?

One is tabby with emerald eyes,
    And a tail that's long and slender,
And into a temper she quickly flies
    If you ever by chance offend her.
        I think we shall call her this —
        I think we shall call her that —
Now don't you think that Pepperpot
    Is a nice name for a cat?

One is black with a frill of white,
    And her feet are all white fur,
If you stroke her she carries her tail upright
    And quickly begins to purr.
        I think we shall call her this —
        I think we shall call her that —
Now don't you think that Sootikin
    Is a nice name for a cat?

One is a tortoiseshell, yellow and black,
    With plenty of white about him —
If you tease him, at once he sets up his back,
    He's a quarrelsome one, ne'er doubt him.
        I think we shall call him this —
        I think we shall call him that —
Now don't you think that Scratchaway
    Is a nice name for a cat?

Our old cat has kittens three
    And I fancy these their names will be —
Pepperpot, Sootikin, Scratchaway — there!
    Were ever kittens with these to compare?
And we call the old mother —
    Now what do you think?
Tabitha Longclaws Tiddley Wink.

Thomas Hood

City Mouse and Garden Mouse

The city mouse lives in a house,
The garden mouse lives in a bower:
He's friendly with the frogs and toads.
And sees the pretty plants in flower.

The city mouse eats bread and cheese,
The garden mouse eats what he can:
We will not grudge him seeds and stocks,
Poor little timid, furry man.

Christina Rossetti

The Cow

The friendly cow, all red and white,
I love with all my heart,
She gives me cream with all her might,
To eat with apple-tart.

She wanders lowing here and there,
And yet she cannot stray,
All in the pleasant open air,
The pleasant light of day;

And blown by all the winds that pass
And wet with all the showers,
She walks among the meadow grass,
And eats the meadow flowers.

Robert Louis Stevenson

Little Trotty Wagtail

Little Trotty Wagtail, he went in the rain,
And tittering, tottering sideways, he ne'er got straight again,
He stopped to get a worm, and looked up to catch a fly,
And then he flew away ere his feathers they were dry.

Little Trotty Wagtail, he waddled in the mud,
And left his little footmarks, trample where he would.
He waddled in the water-pudge, and waggle went his tail,
And chirrupt up his wings to dry upon the garden rail.

Little Trotty Wagtail, you nimble all about,
And in the dimpling water-pudge, you waddle in and out —
Your home is nigh at hand, and in the warm pigsty,
So, little Master Wagtail, I'll bid you a good-bye.

John Clare

The Two Rats

He was a rat, and she was a rat,
    And down in one hole they did dwell,
And both were as black as a witch's cat,
    And they loved one another well.

He had a tail, and she had a tail,
    Both long and curling and fine,
And each said, 'Yours is the finest tail
    In the world excepting mine.'

He smelt the cheese, and she smelt the cheese,
    And they both pronounced it good,
And both remarked it would greatly add
    To the charm of their daily food.

So he ventured out, and she ventured out,
    And I saw them go with pain,
But what befell them I never can tell,
    For they never came back again.

Anon.

If You should meet a Crocodile

If you should meet a crocodile
    Don't take a stick and poke him;
Ignore the welcome in his smile,
    Be careful not to stroke him.
For as he sleeps upon the Nile,
    He thinner gets and thinner;
And whene'er you meet a crocodile
    He's ready for his dinner.

Anon.

Natural History

The Dog will come when he is called,
    The Cat will walk away.
The Monkey's cheek is very bald,
    The Goat is fond of play.
The Parrot is a prate-apace,
    Yet I know not what he says,
The noble Horse will win the race,
    Or draw you in a chaise.

The Pig is not a feeder nice,
    The Squirrel loves a nut,
The Wolf would eat you in a trice,
    The Buzzard's eyes are shut.
The Lark sings high up in the air,
    The Linnet in the tree,
The Swan he has a bosom fair,
    And who so proud as he?

Adelaide O'Keefe

The Frog

Be kind and tender to the Frog,
And do not call him names,
As 'Slimy skin' or 'Polly-wog',
Or otherwise 'Ugly James',
Or 'Gap-a-grin', or 'Toad-gone- wrong',
Or 'Billy Bandy-knees',
The Frog is justly sensitive
To epithets like these.
No animal will more repay
A treatment kind and fair —
At least so lonely people say
Who keep a frog (and, by the way,
They are extremely rare).

Hilaire Belloc

Kindness to Animals

Little children, never give
Pain to things that feel and live,
Let the gentle robin come
For the crumbs you save at home —
As his meat you throw along
He'll repay you with a song —
Never hurt the timid hare
Peeping from her green grass lair,
Let her come and sport and play
On the lawn at close of day —
The little lark goes soaring high
To the bright windows of the sky,
Singing as if 'twere always spring,
And fluttering on an untired wing —
Oh! let him sing his happy song,
Nor do these gentle creatures wrong.

Anon.

I have a Fawn

I have a fawn from Aden's land,
On leafy buds and berries nursed,
And you shall feed him from your hand,
Though he may start with fear at first.
And I will lead you where he lies
For shelter in the noon-day heat,
And you may touch his sleeping eyes,
And feel his little silver feet.

Thomas Moore

The Plaint of the Camel

Canarybirds feed on sugar and seed,
    Parrots have crackers to crunch;
And as for the poodles, they tell me
    the noodles
    Have chicken and cream for their lunch.
But there's never a question
About MY digestion,
    ANYTHING does for me.

Cats, you're aware, can repose in a chair,
    Chickens can roost upon rails;
Puppies are able to sleep in a stable,
    And oysters can slumber in pails.
But no one supposes
A poor Camel dozes.
    ANY PLACE does for me.

Lambs are enclosed where it's never
        exposed,
    Coops are constructed for hens;
Kittens are treated to houses well heated,
    And pigs are protected by pens,
But a Camel comes handy
Wherever it's sandy,
    ANYWHERE does for me.

People would laugh if you rode a giraffe,
    Or mounted the back of an ox;
It's nobody's habit to ride on a rabbit,
    Or try to bestraddle a fox.
But as for a Camel, he's
Ridden by families —
    ANY LOAD does for me.

A snake is as round as a hole in the ground;
    Weasels are wavy and sleek;
And no alligator could ever be straighter
    Than lizards that live in a creek.
But a Camel's all lumpy,
And bumpy, and humpy,
    ANY SHAPE does for me.

Charles Edward Carryl

The Tiger

In the immensity of the jungle
the orange tiger lives.
Silently he moves
and gives
the soft sound of his padded feet
back to the silent night.
The hot wind blows,
the tree tops bend
and sway beneath the cloud grey sky.
And where the water spills
cold from the distant hills,
he crouches low to drink.

Joan E. Cass

Acknowledgments

The Editor and Publishers are grateful to the following for the use of copyright material:

Gerald Duckworth and Company Ltd for 'The Frog' from *The Complete Poems* by Hilaire Belloc: Joan E. Cass for 'The Tiger': William Heinemann Ltd and Doubleday and Company Inc., New York, for 'The Pet Shop' ('Animal Store') by Rachel Field from *Taxis and Toadstools:* Methuen and Company Ltd for 'The Hippopotamus's Birthday' from *The Flattered Flying Fish and Other Poems* by E. V. Rieu: William Morrow and Company Inc., New York, for 'Toucans Two' from *Zoo Doings* by Jack Prelutsky: William Heinemann Ltd and Harper and Row, Publishers, Inc., New York, for 'Sunning' from *Crickety, Cricket: The Best Loved Poems* by James S. Tippett.